THE KU KLUX KLAN

The Hooded Face of Prejudice
in the United States

Written by Raphaël Coune
Translated by Emma Hanna

THE KU KLUX KLAN

KEY INFORMATION

- **Founded:**
  - The first Ku Klux Klan (KKK) was founded in 1865 and was disbanded in 1869.
  - The second incarnation of the KKK was founded in 1915 and was disbanded in 1944.
  - Since 1946, many smaller groups have taken up the banner of the KKK and are still active today.
- **Objectives:** to advocate racial purity and white supremacy, and to protect white, Anglo-Saxon, Protestant Americans from any perceived threat.
- **Notable members:**
  - Nathan Bedford Forrest (1821-1877), lieutenant general in the Confederate Army and the first Grand Wizard of the KKK;
  - William Joseph Simmons (1880-1945), soldier, doctor, teacher for the Methodist Episcopal Church, founder of the second KKK and the secret society's second Grand

Wizard;
  - Hiram Wesley Evans (1881-1966), dentist and Imperial Wizard of the KKK;
  - David Duke (born in 1950), founder of the Knights of the Ku Klux Klan.

INTRODUCTION

Nowadays, the first thing that springs to mind when the KKK is mentioned is the memory of the acts of violence committed against black Americans and against the civil rights movement of the 1960s. However, other facts about the organisation are less well known, such as the fact that it first emerged over a century before the assassination of Martin Luther King (American minister and civil rights activist, 1929-1968). Similarly, it is difficult to reconcile the group's actions with the fact that its origins can be partially traced back to the myth of Southern chivalry and the goal of protecting widows and orphans, and few people realise that the riots of the 1960s, which left such indelible scars on the collective imagination, were far from the most brutal acts of violence perpetrated by the KKK. On the other hand, the scandals and conspiracies that the KKK and the world of American politics were embroiled in during the 1920s have faded somewhat from our memory, as has the fact that President Woodrow Wilson (1856-1924), who was renowned for his role in drafting the Treaty of Versailles (1919) and founding the League of Nations, publically praised the KKK and claimed that they were acting in the country's best interests. Today, it seems difficult to believe that there was once a time when five million Americans claimed to believe in and support white supremacy. So how can all of this be explained? The KKK's name still strikes fear into the hearts of anyone who hears it, but what is the real story of this group, which claims to uphold chivalry and aim to protect widows and orphans, but which has committed countless atrocities, gained a particular reputation for public lynchings, and become synonymous with brutal, active racism?

THE CHANGING FACE OF THE KKK

THE ORIGINS OF THE KKK

The KKK was born in Pulaski, Tennessee, as is indicated by the commemorative plaque which was unveiled in 1921 by John B. Kennedy (1839-1921), who was the only one of the founding members who was still alive at the time. This plaque reads as follows: "Ku Klux Klan organized in this, the law office of Judge Thomas M. Jones, December 24th, 1865. Names of original organizers: Calvin E. Jones. John B. Kennedy. Frank O. McCord. John C. Lester. Richard R. Reed. James R. Crowe." However, the current owner of this building has reversed the plaque to face the wall, so while the plaque remains, and serves as a reminder of the town's history, these words are no longer visible, symbolising the town's present-day rejection of this ideology.

The six founders were old friends and former soldiers in the Confederate army, who found themselves at a loose end when they returned home after four years of intense fighting. It was a mere six months after the end of the Civil War, and with no better ideas for how to occupy their time, the men decided to found a club. Their group did not have any specific goals other than meeting up, echoing the concept of the fraternies which were becoming popular among university students. John B. Kennedy suggested calling this club Kuklos (from the Greek *kuklos*, meaning "circle"). James Crowe then suggested splitting the word in half and replacing "os" with "ux" to form the word *lux* (meaning "light" in Latin). Finally, John Lester pointed out that they were all of Scottish descent and had read Walter Scott's (Scottish novelist, 1771-1832) novels about the legendary clans that had ruled over Scotland in bygone eras. They decided to spell the word "clan" with a "K" for alliterative effect, and the Ku Klux Klan was born.

THE AMERICAN CIVIL WAR

The American Civil War was an armed conflict which lasted from 1861 to 1865, and was fought between the Northern United

States (the Union) and seven Southern states (the Confederacy), which sought to secede from the rest of the country. The Confederates refused to acknowledge the election of Abraham Lincoln (1809-1865) as president because he supported the abolition of slavery. As such, the Southern states declared their independence and fought to defend it, while the Unionist states fought with the goal of keeping the country united.

From early 1866 onwards, the six comrades began meeting up in secret, often at night, and decided to dress up in costumes to make themselves look mysterious and spread terror through the town. After all, they reasoned, what could be more entertaining than giving people a fright? They all draped themselves in sheets, cut pillowcases into hoods to cover their hair, and paraded through the streets of Pulaski at night. Who can say whether the town's inhabitants felt fearful or simply amused as they peered out their windows at this bizarre spectacle? Either way, the six young men were delighted to overhear their neighbours discussing it excitedly the next morning, and their ranks soon swelled to include hundreds of new members who were eager to participate in these midnight patrols. Every night, the members of the KKK filed through the streets, creating the illusion of an army of ghostly invaders. The town's black population were particularly spooked by this sight, as the harsh laws of the time that barred them from receiving an education allowed superstition to run rampant, and a belief sprung up that these sinister figures were the ghosts of Confederate soldiers who had died in the war and had come back to haunt the town.

The members of the KKK gradually came to view their nocturnal gatherings as an outlet for their bitterness towards the people that they held responsible for the war and the Confederates' defeat. They no longer saw their night-time wanderings as a way of causing childish mischief, but as a way of genuinely terrifying the town's black population by making them believe that the spirits of murdered soldiers had come to haunt them. They even started plotting ways of making these scenes more realistic: for example, they demanded buckets of water, which they would then "drink" in a single gulp using a pipe hidden beneath their hoods, or "saluted" by holding up a skeletal hand.

A year after it was founded, the first KKK congress was held in Nashville in January 1867. The KKK's influence had spread considerably throughout the state, and the group was starting to see a need for organisation and structure. As such, the members created an admissions process, established an organisational hierarchy and defined the group's philosophy. The KKK became a secret society, and gained a foothold in all of the Southern states. The position of Grand Wizard was offered to Robert E. Lee (general-in-chief of the Confederate Army, 1807-1870), but he turned the role down on account of his age. In the end, Nathan Bedford Forrest was selected as leader.

| Portrait of Nathan Bedford Forrest

The nature of the group's activities gradually transformed, and their nocturnal jokes and strolls were replaced by intimidation tactics and lynchings. For example, they forced black people to vote for the party that the KKK supported, or outright forbade them to go to vote. Anyone who disobeyed the KKK's orders faced reprisals, which were often shockingly savage, and those who challenged an ideology which painted their race as inferior, whether through their own success or their courage, were the ones who had the most to fear. The KKK had no compunctions about subjecting those who spoke out against their actions to their own brand of "justice", which could take the form of kidnapping, whipping, or even murder. However, this activity did not go unpunished, and within months a number of individuals were arrested on suspicion of belonging to the KKK. In response to this proliferation of violence, Forrest officially dissolved the KKK in 1869, but a handful of local cells remained active.

In 1871, the Supreme Court passed a series of laws known as the Ku Klux Klan Act, which made it illegal for two or more people to hold meetings while wearing disguises and for anyone to deprive a citizen of the United States of their rights. Six years later, the KKK was officially outlawed by order of the Supreme Court, following yet another terrorist attack. Tensions eased, and the federal troops which had been occupying the South since the end of the Civil War were withdrawn the same year.

However, these measures were not enough to dispel the deeply ingrained racism that permeated the United States. From 1875 onwards, the Jim Crow laws were gradually enacted in the Southern states, overturning the constitutional amendments which gave black citizens the right to vote and to coexist with white citizens. Although black men had been granted the right to vote, each state retained jurisdiction over the way that law was enforced. Furthermore, this law did not prevent legislation which imposed racial segregation from being enacted at state level. As a result, a profoundly unequal society was born, in which the black population was shunned by and kept separate from white people. The legal system operated on the principle of "separate but equal" right up until the end of the Second World War (1939-1945), and the KKK gradually stopped operating as racial segregation was imposed.

THE FILM THAT TRIGGERED THE REBIRTH OF THE KKK

As the years went by, the world forgot about the KKK. By the turn of the century, few people still remembered their nocturnal processions and vicious lynchings. The organisation's story could easily have ended there, but in 1915, the KKK was reborn, and became more powerful than ever before. That year, 50 years after the end of the Civil War, a hugely successful film sent shockwaves rippling through the tentative peace that had been established in American society. After reading the novel *The Clansman: a Historical Romance of the Ku Klux Klan* (1905) by Thomas Dixon (1864-1946), which romanticised the KKK's history to the point of glorifying it, the director David W. Griffith (1875-1948) was inspired to create *The Birth of a Nation*, one of the most spectacular films of that era. It tells the story of the Civil War and the Reconstruction Era in the Southern states, but Griffith's narrative also has distinct racist undertones: he even went as far as to attempt to justify the crimes perpetrated by the KKK. However, the film was an immense success, and raked in $60 million in the two years following its release.

| Poster for the film *The Birth of a Nation*, 1915.

William J. Simmons (1880-1945) was one of the people who saw this film, and it left a profound impression on him. He felt that he had received a sacred calling: to revive the KKK. On Thanksgiving evening, he invited his friends and family to follow him, and led them to Stone Mountain on the outskirts of Atlanta, Georgia. The group climbed to the summit, where they found a gigantic cross doused in petrol and a makeshift altar with a Bible, the American flag and a sword sitting on top of it – all of which had been left by Simmons earlier that afternoon. The group donned the disguises worn by the KKK, set the cross alight and listened to Simmons as he declared his intentions to establish a second incarnation of the Ku Klux Klan.

DID YOU KNOW?

In the Middle Ages, Scottish clans used flaming crosses as a means of communication. Although the original KKK never used them, they eventually became one of the group's main symbols after Thomas Dixon's book and the film *The Birth of a Nation* were released.

The reborn KKK soon demonstrated even more

extreme nationalist tendencies than the original organisation. Their goal was no longer just to protect the white race from black people, but to protect "real Americans", or "WASPs" (white Anglo-Saxon Protestants), not just from black people, but also from Catholics, Jews and eventually communists. Furthermore, it was no longer a secret society that acted under cover of darkness, but a legally recognised organisation. By 1917, the new KKK was seen as a vigilante group which helped law enforcement operatives to maintain order. However, the new KKK gained popularity much more slowly than its predecessor, and in 1920, five years after it was revived, it had barely over 2000 members.

| Photograph taken during a gathering of the KKK, circa 1920.

That year, the KKK found new momentum in the form of Edward Y. Clarke (born in 1877) and Mary Elizabeth Tyler (1881-1924). They saw the KKK as a well of untapped potential which needed to be channelled, and believed that Simmons needed their guidance to unlock this potential. As such, they offered him their services as publicists and consultants, and signed a contract which provided Simmons with a weekly salary of $100 and introduced membership fees at a rate of $10. They also suggested commercialising the group's costumes, robes, hoods and other insignia, and the KKK therefore bought Gate City Manufacturing Company so that they could produce these items. Simmons was officially made a colonel, despite having previously shied away from accepting this role. From then on, he was never seen without his two pistols, dagger and bag of cartridges.

DID YOU KNOW?

Gatherings of the second KKK always opened with Simmons, the Grand Wizard, planting his dagger into the middle of the table and bellowing a challenge to black people, Catholics and Jews to come and face him. (Decaux, 1977: 22)

Clarke and Tyler's efforts were immensely successful, and the organisation's ranks had swelled to include over 100 000 members by the end of the year. The key to the couple's success lay in their understanding of the disappointment and disillusionment that plagued the men who had come back from fighting in the First World War (1914-1918) only to then struggle to find work, which led them to believe that all the jobs had been taken by immigrants who had fled Europe during the war and settled in America. Clarke and Tyler also took advantage of the isolationist trend that was sweeping through the United States and used it to construct a programme of aggressive Americanism. The new KKK began to turn in an even more nationalist direction.

In less than a year, they had achieved such success that the KKK had over a million dollars in its coffers. However, history repeated itself, and the organisation's leaders once again found themselves unable to contain the violence of their suddenly numerous followers, who began committing the same atrocities as the original organisation. In addition to direct attacks on people's moral values, they were quick to punish black men who were accused of sleeping with white women, white people who associated with black people, and also doctors who practiced abortion. One new punishment which became popular was to strip the accused naked and cover them in tar and feathers. Their processions became more and more sensational, the violence escalated, and several murders were committed.

Having lost all control of the situation, Clarke advised Colonel Simmons to take Hiram Wesley Evans on as an assistant. Evans eventually ousted Simmons from power and succeeded him as Grand Wizard.

| Photograph of Hiram Wesley Evans during a KKK march in 1926.

By 1924, the movement had become a real political force, and successfully lobbied for the election of eleven governors and nine members of Congress. The next year, they reached the impressive number of over five million members. However, this number would soon be no more than a memory. The press were leading a campaign against the KKK, and published their financial records, as well as information about their crimes. Several accusations were also levelled at some of the highest-ranking members of the KKK. The organisation had gone too far, and most states passed a law banning masks. By 1928, the KKK had shrunk to a few hundred thousand members, and when the Great Depression hit the following year, the dying embers of the organisation were stamped out. Americans had lost their taste for parading through the streets. In 1939, a dispirited Evans passed the torch to James A. Colescott (1897-1950). Soon afterwards, the Second World War broke out, further hindering the KKK's activities. Finally, the national tax authorities cracked down on the group in 1944, by which time they had amassed $685 000 in unpaid taxes, which was the final nail in the coffin of the unified, nationally regulated KKK.

THE KKK TODAY

The KKK made two attempts at a second comeback in 1946 under the leadership of Samuel Green and Sam Roper respectively. However, they never managed to reach the same levels of impact and unity as they had previously. As the first anti-segregation laws were passed and the civil rights movement gained momentum, the same costumes and rituals started to appear once again. However, the law was firmly against them, and each successive government proved more willing to listen to the civil rights movement than the last, which eventually led to the decision to put an end to racial inequality. Several riots broke out between 1956 and 1963 as the fight for equality intensified. During this period, there were a recorded 35 deaths, 44 assaults, 30 house bombings, 8 arson attacks, 4 attempted bombings on schools which had opened their doors to black students, 7 attacks on churches and 4 attacks on synagogues. This time, the Southern states no longer had the option of overturning constitutional amendments and Supreme Court orders, despite the riots.

In 1967, the KKK still numbered 50 000 members, but this number progressively dwindled to just 3000 in 1990. Today, the KKK no longer exists as a single, hierarchical organisation, although there are still many local cells which operate independently and follow their own rules and ideology. These groups claim to be following in the KKK's footsteps, and their numbers have been on the rise again since about 2006. Current estimates regarding the strength and numbers of these groups vary a great deal: while the Southern Poverty Law Center (SPLC) estimates that there are currently 179 active cells, with a total of no more than 6000 members, the Anti-Defamation League (ADL) puts the number of total members nationwide as low as 3000. In any case, the reasons behind the group's recent resurgence can be linked to the evolution of the internet and social media, which facilitate communication and the spread of propaganda, as well as the financial crisis of 2008 and the resulting shifts in the American political landscape.

| Photograph taken during a KKK gathering in 2005.

NOTABLE MEMBERS

NATHAN BEDFORD FORREST, THE FIRST GRAND WIZARD OF THE KKK

Nathan Bedford Forrest was born in Bedford County, Tennessee, in 1821. He had a difficult upbringing, as he was the oldest of 12 siblings and lost his father at the age of 15, after which he had to work to support the rest of the family. He became a slave trader and then a plantation owner, and became moderately wealthy thanks to the booming cotton industry. In 1845 he married Mary Ann Montgomery (1826-1893), with whom he had a son, William, in 1846, and a daughter, Fanny, in 1848.

He took an interest in the local politics of Memphis, and was elected alderman (the equivalent of a modern town councillor) in 1858. He was a highly respected member of the town by the time he enlisted to fight for his state in the Civil War. He used his personal funds to engage a cavalry regiment and this, along with his friends' influence, propelled him from the rank of private to lieutenant colonel. He proved to be a capable leader and tactician in battle, and quickly rose through the ranks to become a lieutenant general. When the war ended, he returned home, freed his slaves, and in later years often spoke out in defence of black Americans.

Forrest was offered the position of Grand Wizard of the KKK by a number of his former comrades in arms from the war. At the time, the organisation was trying to present itself as a brotherhood devoted to protecting the interests of the Southern states, such as looking after women and orphans and contributing to postwar reconstruction efforts. As such, Forrest accepted the position, and spoke at many meetings and conferences throughout the South to highlight what he saw as the problems caused by the abolition of slavery, as well as the losses suffered by the South during the war. His goal was to shape the KKK into a political force which would be capable of serving Southern interests.

In fact, the KKK's first Grand Wizard did not share the deeply ingrained racial prejudice and hatred with which the organisation would later become synonymous. On the contrary, he fought to put an end to the acts of violence committed by members of the organisation, and when he saw that the situation was spiralling out of control, he chose to disband the KKK entirely. In his later years, he publicly criticised the actions of the movement he had once led, and opposed violence towards the black population, stating that the white people behind the attacks were dishonouring themselves.

WILLIAM JOSEPH SIMMONS, THE FOUNDER OF THE SECOND KKK

Little is known about William Joseph Simmons' childhood. He was the son of Calvin Henry Simmons (1836-1893), a doctor from Harpersville, Alabama, and although he had planned to study medicine and follow in his father's footsteps from a young age, he enlisted in the American army to fight in the Spanish-American War (April-August 1898) before finishing his studies. After completing a degree at Johns Hopkins University, he became a teacher for the Methodist Episcopal Church South until 1912, when he was suspended for inefficiency. Three years later, he began working for an insurance company, and joined around a dozen different fraternal organisations.

That same year, Simmons took advantage of the tremendous popularity of the film *The Birth of a Nation* and the anti-Semitic conflict which broke out during the trial of Leo Frank (1884-1915), a Jewish industrialist who was accused of raping and murdering 14-year-old Mary Phagan, to revive the KKK. After declaring himself the Imperial Wizard of the organisation, he began establishing a new hierarchy and ideology for the group. Despite a sluggish, ineffectual beginning, the new KKK's popularity surged when Simmons engaged the services of the professional publicists and communications specialists Edward Y. Clarke and Mary Elizabeth Tyler. In 1922, Simmons was ousted by Hiram W. Evans, who replaced him as leader. Although Simmons launched an appeal against Evans, he never regained his influence or his position in the KKK.

DID YOU KNOW?

Simmons' childhood governess was a black woman, who would often tell him stories about the many sleepless, terrifying nights of her childhood when she feared that the men of the KKK might burst in.

HIRAM WESLEY EVANS, THE IMPERIAL ASSISTANT

Hiram W. Evans was born in Ashland, Alabama, in 1881. He was the son of Martin Evans, a judge, and studied at Vanderbilt University before becoming a dentist. He opened his own practice in the centre of Dallas in 1900, and soon became fairly successful because he charged less than his competitors.

In 1912, he joined the Disciples of Christ, a movement which aimed to unite all Christians behind a single church based on the principles of the New Testament, as well as the Freemasons, and later the KKK in 1920. He was a charismatic speaker and extremely ambitious, which helped him to rise through the ranks of the KKK with astonishing speed. In 1921, Clarke tasked him with supervising the organisation's national recruitment campaigns, which gave him the opportunity to travel and meet with local KKK leaders on a regular basis.

In 1922, he became the leader of a group of militant KKK members who aimed to reorganise the movement's internal structure. This group also included Clarke and D. C. Stephenson (Grand Dragon of the KKK, 1891-1966), who along with Evans were three of the highest-ranking members of the KKK. Evans used the restructuring process to deprive Simmons of most of his power, and Simmons did not resist the coup, as he did not want to stir up discord which could jeopardise the movement. Once he had gained control of the organisation, Evans became embroiled in several disputes with his subordinates, pushing them out in order to ensure that his leadership went uncontested. He also declared his belief in the inherent supremacy of white Anglo-Saxons descended from the first colonists, whom he deemed superior to all other Americans. As a result, he believed that the white race needed to be protected from racial mixing. His ideology, which echoed eugenics theory and scientific racism, both of which were also gaining a foothold at the time, was endorsed by certain important political figures such as the former president Woodrow Wilson, who spoke favourably of the KKK on several public occasions. However, the KKK's popularity soon faded again in spite of Evans' efforts, and in 1939 he ceded his position as leader to James A. Colescott, his former chief of staff, and withdrew from public life.

DAVID DUKE, THE FOUNDER OF THE KNIGHTS OF THE KKK

David Duke was born in Tulsa, Oklahoma in 1950, and his family eventually settled in Louisiana after spending several years travelling around the globe for business reasons during his child-hood. In the 1960s, he met William Luther Pierce (American white supremacist, 1933-2002), the founder of the nationalist, anti-Semitic National Alliance party, who greatly influenced Duke's beliefs.

In 1967, Duke joined the local cell of the KKK, and two years later he founded the White Youth Alliance at Louisiana State University. He was arrested for the first time in 1972, along with three friends, on the charge of inciting a riot.

The skirmish in question broke out after Duke and the others placed a Confederate flag on the Robert E. Lee Monument. A few months later, he founded the Knights of the Ku Klux Klan (KKKK), an organisation which aimed to re-establish racial segregation, and named himself its Imperial Wizard. However, he rejected the group's traditional disguises in favour of a suit and tie, having decided to modernise the old KKK's outdated traditions. In 1976, he organised several Neo-Nazi gatherings in Europe, and helped found a Canadian branch of the KKK. Duke was deported, and gradually distanced himself from the KKKK's activities, especially when several members accused him of misappropriating the group's funds for his personal expenses. Having already campaigned for election to the Louisiana Senate in 1975 and 1979, he left the KKKK in 1980 and devoted himself to politics full-time. He joined the National Association for the Advancement of White People (NAAWP) and ran in the primaries for the Democrat Party in the presidential election of 1988, winning a mere 0.04% of the vote. He then jumped ship to join the Republican Party, and served as an elected member of the Louisiana House of Representatives from 1989 to 1992. In 1991, he campaigned to be elected as Governor of Louisiana, and received a sizeable share of the vote. One year later, he ran in the primaries for the Republican Party in another presidential election, receiving a mere 0.94% of the vote.

This was his last foray into the world of politics until 2016, when he ran in the elections for the US Senate, although he has continued to endorse other candidates from time to time, such as Donald Trump (American president and businessman, born in 1946). He has been deported from Italy and the Czech Republic for incitement to hatred and on suspicion of trying to found a European Neo-Nazi organisation.

AIMS AND OPERATIONS OF THE KKK

ORGANISATIONAL STRUCTURE

The KKK is an extremely hierarchical organisation. Each member is assigned a rank, which dictates their role and goals within the movement, and their outfit and insignia correspond to this rank. The Nashville conference of 1867 and the *Kloran* written by Simmons when he revived the movement have formed the basis for a pseudo-empire which stretches over vast swathes of territory. The KKK also has a security branch, a legal branch, and its own hierarchy, vocabulary and protocols. KKK cells generally follow these provisions, though their local, decentralised nature can lead to a certain degree of disparity.

The hierarchy of the First KKK

Territory	Leadership and administration
The Den (Klan term denoting a town)	A Cyclops assisted by a Grand Exchequer (treasurer), a Grand Mage (second-in-command), a Grand Monk (third-in-command) and two Nighthawks (responsible for communications).
The Provinces (equivalent of counties)	A Grand Giant assisted by four Goblins (councillors), a Grand Exchequer and a Grand Scribe (responsible for lists of members).
The Dominions (equivalent of districts)	A Grand Titan assisted by six Furies (councillors), a Grand Exchequer and a Grand Scribe.
The Realms (the kingdom, equivalent to the State)	A Grand Dragon assisted by eight Hydra (councillors), a Grand Exchequer and a Grand Scribe.
The Empire (the KKK's zone of influence)	A Grand Wizard assisted by ten Genii, an Imperial Exchequer and an Imperial Scribe.

In 1867, the KKK's organisational structure also consisted of Grand Sentinels, who were grouped into Grand Guards and tasked with ensuring the members' safety, as well as a Grand Council of Yahoos, which was assembled and led by the regional Grand Giant and dealt with legal affairs that concerned higher-ranking members of the KKK, and a Grand Council of Centaurs for legal issues concerning the organisation's lower-ranking members. However, it appears that these two councils, which were created during the Nashville conference of 1867, were not active for very long, and were eventually replaced by local tribunals which were organised differently in each region. Finally, the first KKK also included members known as Grand Turks who guided new members through the rites of initiation.

The hierarchy of the Second KKK

Territory	Leader-ship	Assis-tants	Meetings	Attire
The Klanton (town)	Exalted Cyclops or Klavern	12 Terrors	N/A	Black robe and red cowl
The Province (district)	Titan	Seven Furies	Klonverse	White robe, green cowl and four green chevrons on the sleeves
The Realm	Grand Dragon	Nine Hydra	Klorero	Green robe
The Empire	Grand Wizard/ Imperial Wizard/ Imperial Assistant	The Imperial Kloncil-ium (15 Genii)	Klonvo-cation	Purple robe

Simmons used his *Kloran* to take the tradition of inventing vocabulary even further. Gatherings were given different names to denote their scope, and each ranking member was given a title which made their role within the organisation clear.

The adjectives "Grand" and "Imperial" were also introduced as a way of distinguishing between different ranks. As such, the Imperial Klabee was the Empire-level treasurer, a Grand Klabee was a Realm-level treasurer, and each Great Klabee was a Province-level treasurer.

Roles as defined by Simmons in the *Kloran*

Title	Role	Title	Role
Kleagle	Recruiter	Klabee	Treasurer
Klaliff	Vice-President	Kladd	Conductor (in charge of initiating new members)
Klokard	Lecturer	Klarogo	Inner guard
Kludd	Chaplain	Klexter	Outer guard
Kligrapp	Secretary	Night-hawk	Communications officer

The procedures for joining up remained more or less identical from the first KKK to the second. Anyone could act as a recruiter, working for the Kleagle of each Klanton, especially under the second KKK, when each recruiter received a $4 commission for each new member. Aspiring new members were gathered together at night and had to answer ten questions. If they answered "yes" to each one, they were judged worthy of joining the movement. This list of questions included:

- Are you a good citizen?
- Are you American?
- Are you a good Christian?
- Are you of Anglo-Saxon descent?
- Are you opposed to racial equality?

OPERATIONS

During the Nashville conference, the KKK defined itself as "an institution of chivalry, humanity, mercy, and patriotism; embodying in its genius and its principles all that is chivalric". This conference also established the movement's three main goals: firstly, to protect the innocent from the indignities and outrages of the lawless, the violent, and the brutal, and to provide for the needy, especially the widows and orphans of Confederate soldiers. Secondly, to defend the Constitution of the United States, and all laws passed in accordance with it, and to protect the states against any invasion. Finally, to aid in the enforcement of all constitutional laws. These may seem like noble goals, but the consequences they led to speak for themselves.

As we can see from the group's stated goals, they initially hoped to protect widows from the aggressive behaviour they believed black men would exhibit towards them, having just been freed from slavery, and to protect the Southern states from invaders from the Northern states who looked at the war-torn, poverty-stricken South and saw a chance to make some easy money. However, the focus of these aims soon warped and twisted into something else entirely: white women were still "protected", but rather than aiding those who had been left without the means to protect themselves, this "protection" soon came to be synonymous with ensuring racial purity. The KKK believed that freeing black slaves threatened white supremacy and racial purity, and that this meant that any actions they undertook to bolster white supremacy were in line with the group's founding principles.

KKK members gathering in full costume in public locations or in areas which were popular with the black population became a common practice, as did demonstrations and marches. Parading through the streets in costume became their favoured way of affirming their power and intimidating those around them. One aspect of the KKK's strategy was to make as many public appearances as possible in order to give non-members the impression that everyone was part of the KKK and that no one would bat an eye if they joined up too. The group's largest processions included a march which took place in Indiana on 4 July 1923 in which 200 000 people took part, and two parades which took place in Washington in August 1925 and 1926, with 30 000 and 40 000 people marching in them respectively.

| Photograph of a KKK parade through Washington, 1926.

But of course, the KKK did not become one of the most notorious organisations in the world through their law-abiding actions. Members of the KKK gathered together in secret, under cover of night, or in disguise to commit a series of atrocities: public lynchings, tarring, humiliation, branding their victims with the bright red letters "KKK", kidnappings and assassinations. Some members of the police and the authorities were in league with the KKK, while others simply failed to grasp just how powerful the organisation was, and failed to take adequate measures to counter their actions. It was only when the desegregation process began in the 1960s that the US federal government began systematically opposing institutions which refused to obey these laws, which often triggered riots led by members of the KKK. American society was deeply horrified by the extent of the violence that characterised these demonstrations.

The KKK also engaged in less physical pursuits, such as conferences held by Klokards where members' theses could be discussed, and the creation of an organisation-wide newspaper. Finally, the KKK was also active in politics. Members of the group often lobbied for or against various bills, laws and election candidates. This approach proved successful in 1924, when several members of the KKK were elected as governors or members of Congress. Politicians were also well aware of the extent of the organisation's influence, and certain figures actually joined the group in order to secure enough votes to be re-elected.

DID YOU KNOW?

Harry S. Truman (1944-1972), who was elected president of the United States in 1945, joined the KKK in 1924 to ensure that he would be re-elected as a judge in Kansas. He was an inactive member, and left a few months later after being ordered to refrain from hiring any Catholics or Jews.

CONTROVERSIES

The KKK's history is a tapestry of controversy, scandal and clashes with the law. However, there are four particular affairs which are worth describing briefly here, as they had repercussions at a national level and a significant negative impact on the movement. The first three incidents took place during the early 1920s and are generally considered to be the main driving forces behind the movement's decline. The fourth incident was more recent, and reflects the way modern organisations which claim to be following in the KKK's footsteps have idealised the Confederate South and its symbols.

THE DANIEL AND RICHARDS AFFAIR

In early summer 1922, Dr B. M. McKoin, the Exalted Cyclops and former mayor of the town of Mer Rouge in Louisiana, claimed that his car was shot at while he was returning from a round of visits. The local branch of the KKK rallied around him and immediately arrested two of its opponents, Watt Daniel (died in 1922) and Tom

Richards (died in 1922), his mechanic. The two men were released due to lack of evidence, but while they were being arrested, they recognised several members of the KKK in spite of the disguises they were wearing.

The KKK realised that they had been compromised when the two young men told their friends and families all about their ordeal, and identified some of the men who had arrested them. Soon, everyone knew about the incident. The local KKK gathered again on 22 August 1922 and blocked the main road into the town with a lorry in order to find the two men. Once they had been located, they were kidnapped and taken to a clearing outside the town, where they were whipped to death.

This incident was taken very seriously by the local authorities, as this was the first time the KKK had been responsible for the death of white Catholics. Lake Lafourche was scoured by professional divers and two mutilated bodies were found a few days later. The police arrested several members of the KKK, who admitted to flagellating the victims but denied all charges of murder. The judge, who had to hire armed men to ensure that members of the KKK were kept out of the courtroom, was eventually compelled to acquit the accused of all charges. This incident scandalised American society, and public opinion turned firmly against the KKK, but it also had repercussions within the movement, as Grand Wizard Simmons was criticised for failing to take action.

EDWARD CLARKE'S CLASHES WITH THE LAW

No one could ever claim that Edward Clarke, the man who helped the second KKK to gain a national platform, was above reproach. The numerous legal scandals he was embroiled in gradually tarnished the public image of the KKK, which was still claiming to be a chivalrous organisation which aimed to protect and purify the Anglo-Saxon race.

In 1919, the future Imperial Kleagle's wife filed for divorce on grounds of desertion after she caught him in a compromising position with his colleague Mary Elizabeth Tyler. In 1922, during Prohibition, he was arrested for possession of alcohol on two occasions. In March 1924, he was found guilty of breaking the Mann Act, which prohibited the transportation of a woman or girl from one state to another for the purpose of prostitution or debauchery. He was eventually forced to leave the KKK and to flee the country in order to avoid being brought to justice.

THE STEPHENSON TRIAL

No one could boast of having recruited more members of the KKK than David Curtis Stephenson (1891-1966), a well-known Indiana politician who eventually became the Grand Dragon of the KKK. Between 1922 and 1923, he recruited 2000 new members in his consti-tuency each week. His tremendous popularity allowed him to amass a spectacular fortune and significant power, while his wealth of political connections proved a valuable asset for the KKK. Emboldened by his success, he decided to cut ties with the Imperial Wizard, who at that time was Hiram Wesley Evans, and with the national KKK, setting up the KKK chapters that he was in charge of as an independent organisation. His ambitions were growing ever-grander, and he was hoping to launch a political career.

Everything changed when Madge Oberholtzer (1896-1925) was found dead, having contracted a staphylococcal infection from bites Stephenson had left on her chest, and from having attempted suicide by drinking mercury chloride. Stephenson had kidnapped her, raped her and inflicted multiple injuries on her. The young teacher left a suicide note describing this ordeal, and how Stephenson refused to get her medical treatment unless she agreed to marry him. Autopsy reports showed that he could have saved her life by getting her the care she needed in time. A trial was launched, and Stephenson was sentenced to life imprisonment for multiple counts of rape, torture, and second degree murder.

This scandal rocked the KKK, which felt indignant that one of its heroes had committed such a heinous act, and led a massive decline in membership. While in prison, Stephenson asked his old friend, Edward Jackson (1873-1954), who was the Governor of Indiana at the time, to pardon him, but this request was refused. Feeling betrayed, he published a list of public officials who had accepted bribes from the KKK, leading to the downfall of many other public figures, including Governor Jackson, the leader of the Republican Party for Marion County, the mayor of Indianapolis, and several Republican commissioners.

TAKING DOWN THE CONFEDERATE FLAG IN SOUTH CAROLINA

On 18 June 2015, South Carolina was rocked by a mass shooting committed by Dylann Roof (born in 1994) in a church in the African-American community in Charleston. Prior to the shooting, Roof (who was 21 at the time) had posted several photos on social media which showed him posing with firearms in front of a Confederate flag. The flag, which over time had come to be seen as a symbol of racism, was still flown in front of the South Caroline State House at that time, and on 10 July the decision was therefore made to remove it.

That day, around a hundred members of Black Educators for Justice marched in support of the state's decision to take the flag down. However, they were soon joined by dozens of protestors from local cells of the KKK, who were brandishing Confederate and Nazi flags. Several skirmishes broke out, so when the flag was eventually taken down by a sizeable deployment of state police, a tremendous clamour could be heard from the watching crowd.

This incident reflects the extent to which the KKK has idealised the notion of a Confederate South, and the importance it places on the symbols associated with it. This mythical Confederate South is imagined as a wealthy land, where the black population would be enslaved, and the members of the KKK are fighting to hold on to the flickering vestiges of this invented memory at any cost.

SUMMARY

- The Ku Klux Klan was founded by six young men who had just returned home from fighting in the American Civil War. It was initially conceived as a mere respite from boredom, modelled after university fraternities.
- The group did not become a real organisation until the Nashville conference of 1867, when it adopted an ideology and a purpose. The KKK's stated goals were to protect widows and orphans and to protect the (Southern) states against invasion. However, this ideology was soon warped to justify the KKK's early attacks against black people, whom they believed to be the cause of the Civil War and a threat to the South.
- The attacks committed by the group and the resulting legal repercussions quickly spiralled out of control, leading to the KKK being officially disbanded in 1869. However, the KKK still cast a hooded shadow across the land for several years, only truly disappearing after the Ku Klux Klan Act (1871) was passed, the

remainder of the occupying troops from the Northern states withdrew from the South and the Jim Crow laws (1875) established racial segregation.

- In 1915, the KKK was revived by William J. Simmons, who had been inspired by a film which cast the first KKK's actions in a favourable light. The new KKK took a more nationalist stance than its predecessor and added Catholics and Jews to its list of enemies, viewing them as invaders who threatened the purity of the white, Protestant, Anglo-Saxon race.

- The KKK reached its apogee in 1925, when it numbered over five million members and had become a real political force which wielded influence at a national level. Governors and senators were elected thanks to KKK influence, and in certain states it became so influential that the majority of the state-level government employees were members, which allowed the group to wreak havoc without fear of reprisals. The KKK was at its strongest during this era, but the organisation's most scandalous legal battles also arose during this period, and eventually led to the group being disbanded again in 1944.

- Despite several attempts, the KKK was never truly reborn after this. Many local cells, which act more or less independently, pop up from time to time, but they bear very little resemblance to the unified national movement that once cast a shadow across the breadth of the United States. The KKK has been locked in a downward spiral since the 1960s, and today nothing remains of the group but a few scattered associations and local clubs, which all have their own wildly disparate rules, rituals and goals.
- Nonetheless, there has been a certain shift in the way these groups operate since 2006, mainly because of the rise of the internet, social media and the financial crisis of 2008. Although the KKK only had around 3000 members in 1990, some current estimates now put their numbers as high as 6000 members in 179 active cells.
- Although the KKK has changed a great deal over the years, particularly with regard to its size, scope, operations and internal structure, the typical mindset of its members never seems to evolve. Whether their hosti-

lity is being directed towards black people, Catholics, Jews, communists or, more recently, Muslims, their aim is always to protect "pure-blood" Americans, and their understanding of what constitutes "purity" is exactly the same as it was 150 years ago, even though society has undergone profound changes since then. Unless they can break free of the twin toxic attitudes of prejudice towards anyone who is different and the need to feel superior to those around them, these attitudes will presumably remain stagnant and unchanging for another 150 years to come.

We want to hear from you!
Leave a comment on your online library
and share your favourite books on social media!

FURTHER READING

BIBLIOGRAPHY

- Chalmers, D. (1987) *Hooded Americanism: The History of the Ku Klux Klan*. Durham, North Carolina: Duke University Press.

- Decaux, A. (1977) Les cagoulards du KKK. *Historia*. Paris: Librairie Jules Tallandier. pp. 14-25.

- Fry, H. (1969) *The Modern Ku Klux Klan*. New York: Negro Universities Press.

- Hodgson, G. (1966) *Carpetbaggers et Ku-Klux Klan. Les États-Unis après la guerre de Sécession*. Paris: Gallimard.

- Kaspi, A. (1993) *Les 1 000 jours d'un président*. Paris: Armand Colin.

- Kaspi, A. (1994) *Les États-Unis au temps de la prospérité (1919-1929)*. Paris: Fayard.

- Kennedy, S. (1958) *J'ai appartenu au Ku Klux Klan*. Paris: Morgan.

- Lester, J. and Wilson, D. (1905) *Ku Klux Klan: Its Origin, Growth and Disbandment*. New York: Washington Neale.

- Newton, M. (2006) *The Ku Klux Klan: History, Organization, Language, Influence and Activities of*

America's Most Notorious Secret Society. Jefferson: McFarland & Company.

- Portes, J. (1988) *L'âge doré (1865-1896).* Nancy: Presses universitaires de Nancy.

- Randel, W. (1965) *The Ku Klux Klan: A Century of Infamy.* Philadelphia: Chilton Books.

- Trelease, A. (1972) *White Terror: The Ku Klux Klan Conspiracy and Southern Reconstruction.* New York: Harper Torchbooks.

- Wyn Craig, W. (1998) *The Fiery Cross: The Ku Klux Klan in America.* Oxford: Oxford University Press.

ICONOGRAPHIC SOURCES

- Portrait of Nathan Bedford Forrest. Royalty-free reproduction image.

- Poster for the film *The Birth of a Nation*, 1915. Royalty-free reproduction image.

- Photograph taken during a gathering of the KKK, circa 1920. Royalty-free reproduction image.

- Photograph of Hiram Wesley Evans during a KKK march in 1926. Royalty-free reproduction image.

- Photograph taken during a KKK gathering in 2005. Royalty-free reproduction image.

- Photograph of a KKK parade through Washington, 1926. Royalty-free reproduction image.

FILMS

- *The Birth of a Nation.* (1915) [Film]. David Wark Griffith. Dir. USA: Epoch Producing Co.

- *Mississippi Burning.* (1988) [Film]. Alan Parker. Dir. USA: Orion Pictures.

LITERATURE

- Dixon, T. (1905) *The Clansman: A Historical Romance of the Ku Klux Klan.* New York: Doubleday.

- Dixon, T. (1939) *The Flaming Sword.* Atlanta: Monarch Publishing.

COMMEMORATIVE BUILDINGS

- Cathedral of Christ the King, the KKK's former headquarters in Atlanta, Georgia.

- Commemorative plaque for the first KKK in Pulaski, Tennessee.

IMPROVE YOUR GENERAL KNOWLEDGE

IN A BLINK OF AN EYE !

www.50minutes.com

www.50minutes.com

Ebook EAN: 9782808002509

Paperback EAN: 9782808002516

Legal Deposit: D/2017/12603/646

Cover: © Primento

Digital conception by Primento, the digital partner of publishers.